P9-DCC-158

Someone I Love Died

Written by
Christine Harder Tangvald

Illustrated by
Victoria Ponikvar

Equipping Kids for Life!
faithkids.com

A Faith Parenting Guide
at back of book

With praise to Jesus and glory to God,
I dedicate this book to:
My wonderful parents, Harry and Frankie Harder,
And to my beloved son, Thor Roald Tangvald.

They have already crossed the chasm and are
experiencing the reality of eternal life.
Wait for me. Wait for me.

Faith Kids® is an imprint of
Cook Communications Ministries, Colorado Springs, CO 80918
Cook Communications, Paris, Ontario
Kingsway Communictions, Eastbourne, England

SOMEONE I LOVE DIED
© 1988 by Christine Harder Tangvald

All rights reserved. No part of this book may be reproduced without written permission,
except for brief quotations in books and critical reviews. For information, write Cook Communications Ministries, 4050 Lee Vance View,
Colorado Springs, CO 80918.

This edition first printed in 2002.
Printed in Singapore
2 3 4 5 6 7 8 9 10 Printing/Year 06 05 04 03 02

Editor: Phyllis Williams
Designed by: Dana Sherrer
Illustrated by: Victoria Ponikvar

Unless otherwise noted, Scripture quotations are taken from the Holy Bible: New International
Version®. Copyright © 1973, 1978, 1984 by International Bible Society. Used by permission of
Zondervan Publishing House. All rights reserved.

ISBN 1-55513-490-4

$\mathcal{S}$omeone I know who died is _____ .
(I liked _____ a lot.)

Some people think when a person dies, that is the end of every-thing. But they are wrong, aren't they? That's not how God works at all.

You see, God has a plan:
> a plan for *life*
>> a plan for *death*
>>> and a plan for *life after death*.

But thinking about death can be sort of sad and upsetting, can't it?

And there are lots of things about death that are hard to understand.

Let's start at the beginning. Did you know that a long time ago, God created the body for the very first man out of the dust of the earth?

He did.

God created people special—different from the animals. He made people a lot like himself—in God's own image.

God breathed into the man's body the *breath of life,* and man became a living soul.

Genesis 1:27; 2:7

*W*hen one of God's people dies, God moves the breath of life back *out* of the body to a special place we call *heaven,* a place we can't see right now.

It's true!

A very important part of the person *does not die ... ever!* That is the part that we call the *soul*—the part that lived inside the body—the part that makes us laugh and cry and listen and feel and pray and think.

That part of the person has moved to heaven to live with Jesus forever and ever and ever.

And not only that, but guess who likes it in heaven? Guess who *loves* it in heaven?

_____ does! Because heaven is a place filled with *joy.*

Matthew 5:12

So when a person dies, the body is like an empty house. Nobody lives in there anymore.

Since it isn't needed anymore, we put the body in a large box called a casket and bury it in the ground. But it's okay, because the soul moved out and is already happy in heaven.

Understanding this is hard, but it's all a part of God's plan.

One question I have is _____ .

For the person who died, it is the end of life here on earth, but it is the beginning of life in heaven.

It's sort of like the person has a new birthday in heaven—a new beginning. And just like our birthday here is a very happy day for us, their birthday in heaven is a very happy day, too.

But do *you* feel happy when someone dies? _____.

If the person in heaven is happy, then why aren't *we* happy?

It doesn't seem fair. We wish the person who died could come back and stay here with us. But that can't happen. It just can't.

So we are lonely and we feel really *upset*. It's okay to feel upset. In fact, it's okay to feel any way you feel.

Some people feel sad or angry.

Some people don't.

Some people feel lonely or scared.

Some people don't.

And some people don't know exactly how they feel, except that they are really upset.

However you feel is okay. You might want to cry and cry. Sometimes it feels good to cry. Crying is another way to say, "I love you."

Right now I feel _____ .

But I will feel better again after a while. I will be happy again. Maybe I don't think so right now, but it will happen.

I won't feel so sad and lonely. And I won't be so sad. I'll start to smile again and then even laugh.

I might even play and _____ .

Maybe not right now, but later.

I will.

But I want to tell someone how I feel right now! Who can I talk to when I'm upset?

I can talk to Mom and Dad, to my friends, to my pastor, to _____ and _____ .

But it's especially good to talk to God when we are upset. God understands. He knows we don't want someone we love to die.

Sometimes we need to talk to God even if we don't really want to. We can tell God *exactly* how we feel right now.

Something I am sad or upset about is _____ .
Something I want to *ask* God is _____ .
Something I want to *tell* God is _____ .

Sometimes when we talk to God it gives us a calm, quiet feeling inside called *peace.* We feel safer and stronger when we trust God.

*P*eople can die when they are young or when they are old or at any age in between. It's not their fault when they die. Another thing I *know* is that it is *not my fault* when someone dies.

Some things that cause people to die are:

Accidents
Getting old
Diseases
_____

The person that I know died from _____.

I wonder how people get to go to heaven?

Oh, this is the *best* part of God's plan. Jesus is the one who opens the door to heaven. Jesus invites everyone in.

God sent his own Son, Jesus, to be our Savior. Jesus lived here on earth. Jesus died here on earth. And Jesus was raised up from being dead. Now he lives in heaven. It was a miracle!

*W*hen we accept Jesus as our personal friend and Savior, all our sins are forgiven, and he opens the door for us to heaven.

And *everyone* is invited!

_____ is invited, too.

Jesus said: "I am the resurrection and the life. He who believes in me will live, even though he dies; and whoever lives and believes in me will never die. Do you believe this?" (John 11:25)

Is Jesus your personal friend and Savior? _____

Thank you, Jesus, for opening the door to heaven for me and for _____ .

Ephesians 2:8; Isaiah 61:10–62:3

Another thing I want to know is, how fast does a person's soul go to heaven?

faster than you can clap your hands
faster than you can stomp your feet
faster than you can say your name

That is how fast the soul goes to heaven when a person dies.

Jesus told one man, "Today you will be with me in paradise." (Luke 23:43)

Today means right away.

I wonder *where* heaven is and *what* it is like? Are there stars in heaven, and flowers and trees and animals and sunshine? Does it rain in heaven? Will there be rainbows?

I hope so, don't you? But we really don't know. We don't know exactly where heaven is or what it is like. But we don't have to know, because God knows.

But we do know heaven is wonderful. It is not a sad or scary place to be. It is a *happy* place, a *fun* place, a *terrific* place. In fact, heaven is better than the very best place you can think of.

Jesus said so. He said, "In my Father's house are many rooms ... I am going there to prepare a place for you." (John 14:2)

We can trust Jesus' promise because Jesus never ever lies. Never! Ever!

Heaven is one of the best parts of God's plan.

I think heaven is _____ .

And guess who is already there! Lots of people are already in heaven. You probably know some of them.

FAMILY:

1. _____ 2. _____

FRIENDS:

1. _____ 2. _____

Lots of people from the Bible are already in heaven, like:

Abraham and Moses
Matthew, Mark, Luke, and John
Mary and Martha

_____ and _____

And aren't there angels in heaven? There certainly are. *Lots* of them.

I wonder how many people are already in heaven?

I wonder what they are doing right now?

Here's a picture of what I think heaven might be like.

Revelation 7:9, 10

Aren't you glad God has a plan? A plan of hope and joy.

Here are some things I know:

It is not my fault if someone dies.

It is okay to feel however I feel.

The person who died is just fine. The soul moved out of the body to a special place we call heaven.

Jesus opens the door to heaven and everyone is invited in.

Heaven is not a sad or scary place. Heaven is wonderful ... a place of joy. Jesus said so.

God will help me through sad, hard times, and sometime later I will feel happy again.

Someday, all God's people will meet with Jesus in heaven. That will be a happy, happy day.

Thank you, God, for your plan.

Something I am glad about is _____ .

PRAYER

Dear God,

Hi, it's me, _____ .

Thank you for your plan, God. Thank you for life here on earth and for life in heaven.

Thank you for making heaven safe and happy so I don't have to worry.

God, I want to feel safe and happy, too. Please help me when I'm sad. Help me when I'm lonely or mad. And help me if I get upset.

I'm so glad to know I will feel better again—after a while.

Thank you, Jesus, for being my very own friend and Savior. Thank you for opening the door to heaven. You are the most important part of God's plan ... and mine!

Knowing about this makes me feel better. Lots better. But if I have more questions and mixed-up feelings, I will be talking to you again, God.

Real soon.

AMEN

For God so loved the world that he gave his one and only Son, that whoever believes in him shall not perish but have eternal life.

John 3:16

Faith
Parenting
Guide

Ages
3and up

Hope

Someone I Love Died

Spiritual Building Block: Hope

Life Issue: My children need to develop confidence
that God will fulfill his promises to us.

Help your children learn about hope in the following ways:

 Sight. Explain step by step the procedures for what is going to
happen now, and some of the words that children will be hearing,
such as casket, viewing the body, funeral, cemetery, grave, soul,
Heaven, God, and Jesus. This will help your children to avoid any
unpleasant and surprising experiences. Pray together as a family,
and accept prayers and support from your family, friends, church,
and most of all from God. When children experience the love of oth-
ers through a time of grief, they begin to learn that God hears and
understands how we feel.

Sound. Encourage children to talk openly about how they feel.
Listen to what they are really saying. Do not be judgmental if they
do not act or respond as you think they should. Answer their questions honestly, but don't go into more detail than is needed or can be
understood. Make sure your children understand the cause of death,
and that nothing they have said or wished or done has contributed
to the person's death in any way. Death often makes us feel helpless
and vulnerable. Talking out our feelings is an excellent therapy.

Touch. Give children your time and attention so they don't feel left out. Permit them to participate, but don't force them to. Physical reassurance is essential. Hug your children, hold hands, and remember to make frequent eye contact. Just a wink or a nod of your head can give children comfort and alleviate the fear of being abandoned. Assure your children that what happened to the friend or family member is not going to happen to them—or to you. And remember to give your children opportunities to play with other children to escape the constant feelings of sadness that can surround a death.